Traveling to New Communities

Senior Authors
Roger C. Farr
Dorothy S. Strickland

Authors
Richard F. Abrahamson ♦ Alma Flor Ada ♦ Barbara Bowen Coulter
Bernice E. Cullinan ♦ Margaret A. Gallego
W. Dorsey Hammond
Nancy Roser ♦ Junko Yokota ♦ Hallie Kay Yopp

Senior Consultant
Asa G. Hilliard III

Consultants
Kanani Choy ♦ Lee Bennett Hopkins ♦ Stephen Krashen ♦ Rosalia Salinas

Harcourt Brace & Company
Orlando Atlanta Austin Boston San Francisco Chicago Dallas New York Toronto London

Copyright © 1997 by Harcourt Brace & Company. All rights reserved. ISBN 0-15-308323-9
1 2 3 4 5 6 7 8 9 10   048   99 98 97 96

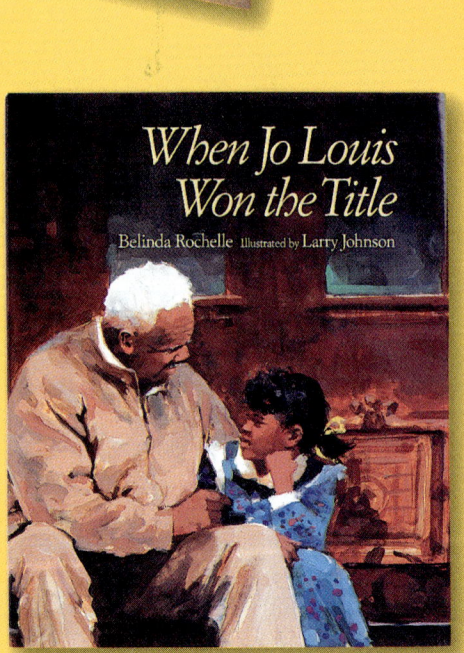

Traveling to New Communities

CONTENTS

110 Theme Opener

112 Bookshelf

Biography/Social Studies

114 **My Great-Aunt Arizona**
*by Gloria Houston
illustrated by Susan Condie Lamb*

Profile: Gloria Houston and Susan Condie Lamb

Autobiographical Story/Social Studies

130 **Grandfather's Journey**
written and illustrated by Allen Say

Profile: Allen Say

Poem

162 **That Mountain Far Away**
Traditional Tewa Poem

Poem

163 **Travel**
by Edna St. Vincent Millay

Historical Fiction/Social Studies

166 **The Lotus Seed**
*by Sherry Garland
illustrated by Tatsuro Kiuchi*

Profile: Sherry Garland

Art

188 **Art and Literature:**
*The Bay and Harbor of New York
by Samuel B. Waugh*

Realistic Fiction/Social Studies

190 **Amber Brown Is Not a Crayon**
*by Paula Danziger
illustrated by Tony Ross*

Profile: Paula Danziger

Realistic Fiction/Social Studies

202 **When Jo Louis Won the Title**
*by Belinda Rochelle
illustrated by Larry Johnson*

Profile: Belinda Rochelle and Larry Johnson

220 Theme Wrap-Up

333 Glossary

9

• THEME •

Traveling to New Communities

CONTENTS

My Great-Aunt Arizona
by Gloria Houston

Grandfather's Journey
written and illustrated by Allen Say

That Mountain Far Away
Traditional Tewa Poem

Travel
by Edna St. Vincent Millay

The Lotus Seed
by Sherry Garland

Art and Literature:
The Bay and
Harbor of New York
by Samuel B. Waugh

**Amber Brown Is
Not a Crayon**
by Paula Danziger

**When Jo Louis
Won the Title**
by Belinda Rochelle

Bookshelf

Dandelions
by Eve Bunting

When Zoe realizes that her mother misses the city she grew up in, she does something to make her mother feel more at home on the prairie.

Award-Winning Author and Illustrator
Signatures Library

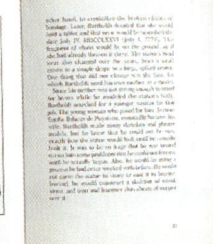

The Statue of Liberty
by Jim Haskins

America's "proud lady" has greeted countless immigrants with the promise of freedom.

Award-Winning Author
Signatures Library

Halmoni and the Picnic
by Sook Nyul Choi

Yunmi's third-grade class helps her grandmother feel comfortable in the United States.

Back Home
by Gloria Jean Pinkney

A city girl from the North learns about farm life in the South when she visits her mother's relatives.

ALA Notable Book; Notable Trade Book in Social Studies; Award-Winning Illustrator

Amber Brown Goes Fourth
by Paula Danziger

Amber's best friend has moved. Who will help her face fourth grade?

Award-Winning Author

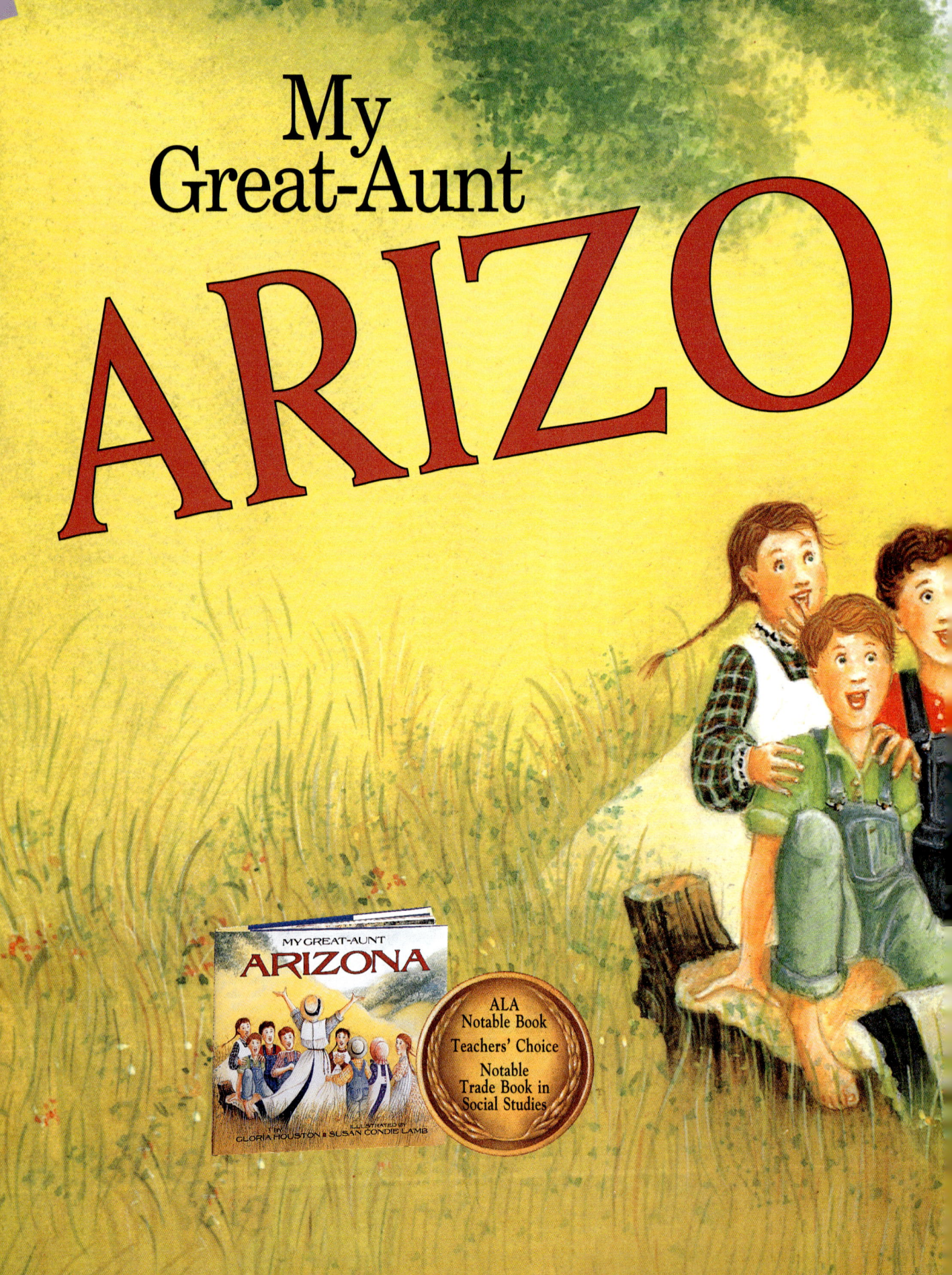

My great-aunt Arizona was born in a log cabin her papa built in the meadow on Henson Creek in the Blue Ridge Mountains. When she was born, the mailman rode across the bridge on his big bay horse with a letter.

The letter was from her brother, Galen, who was in the cavalry, far away in the West. The letter said, "If the baby is a girl, please name her Arizona, and she will be beautiful, like this land."

Arizona was a very tall little girl. She wore her long brown hair in braids. She wore long full dresses, and a pretty white apron. She wore high-button shoes, and many petticoats, too. Arizona liked to grow flowers.

She liked to read, and sing, and square dance to the music of the fiddler on Saturday night.

Arizona had a little brother, Jim. They played together on the farm. In summer they went barefoot and caught tadpoles in the creek.

In the fall they climbed the mountains searching for galax and ginseng roots.

In the winter they made snow cream with sugar, snow, and sweet cream from Mama's cows. When spring came, they helped Papa tap the maple trees and catch the sap in buckets. Then they made maple syrup and maple-sugar candy.

Arizona and her brother Jim walked up the road that wound by the creek to the one-room school. All the students in all the grades were there, together in one room. All the students read their lessons aloud at the same time. They made a great deal of noise, so the room was called a blab school.

The students carried their lunches in lard buckets made of tin. They brought ham and biscuits. Sometimes they had fried apple pie. They drank cool water from the spring at the bottom of the hill. At recess they played games like tag and William Matrimmatoe.

When Arizona had read all the books at the one-room school, she crossed the mountains to the school in another village, a village called Wing. It was so far away that she rode her papa's mule. Sometimes she rode the mule through the snow.

When Arizona's mother died, Arizona had to leave school and stay home to care for Papa and her brother Jim. But she still loved to read—and dream about the faraway places she would visit one day. So she read and she dreamed, and she took care of Papa and Jim.

Then one day Papa brought home a new wife. Arizona could go away to school, where she could learn to be a teacher. Aunt Suzie invited Arizona to live at her house and help with the chores. Aunt Suzie made her work very hard. But at night Arizona could study—and dream of all the faraway places she would visit one day.

Finally, Arizona returned to her home on Henson Creek. She was a teacher at last.

She taught in the one-room school where she and Jim had sat. She made new chalkboards out of lumber from Papa's sawmill, and covered them with polish made for shoes. She still wore long full dresses and a pretty white apron. She wore high-button shoes and many petticoats, too. She grew flowers in every window. She taught students about words and numbers and the faraway places they would visit someday.

"Have you been there?" the students asked.

"Only in my mind," she answered. "But someday you will go."

Arizona married the carpenter who helped build the new Riverside School down where Henson Creek joins the river. So Miss Arizona became Mrs. Hughes, and for the rest of her days she taught fourth-grade students who called her "Miz Shoes."

And when her daughter was born, Miz Shoes brought the baby to school, to the sunny room where flowers grew in every window.

Every year Arizona had a Christmas tree growing in a pot. The girls and boys made paper decorations to brighten up the tree. Then they planted their tree at the edge of the school yard, year after year, until the entire playground was lined with living Christmas trees, like soldiers guarding the room where Arizona taught, with her long gray braids wound 'round her head, with her long full dress, and pretty white apron, with her high-button shoes, and many petticoats, too.

The boys and girls who were students in her class had boys and girls who were students in her class. And they had boys and girls who were students in her class.

For fifty-seven years my great-aunt Arizona hugged her students. She hugged them when their work was good, and she hugged them when it was not. She taught them words and numbers, and about the faraway places they would visit someday.

"Have you been there?" the students asked.

"Only in my mind," she answered. "But someday you will go."

My great-aunt Arizona taught my dad, Jim's only son. And she taught my brother and me in the fourth grade. With her soft white braids wound 'round her head, she taught us about faraway places we would visit someday.

My great-aunt Arizona died on her ninety-third birthday. But she goes with me in my mind—A very tall lady, in a long full dress, and a pretty white apron, with her high-button shoes, and her many petticoats, too. She's always there, in a sunny room with many flowers in every window, and a hug for me every day.

She never did go to the faraway places she taught us about. But my great-aunt Arizona travels with me and with those of us whose lives she touched....

She goes with us in our minds.

Gloria Houston

Gloria Houston, like her great-aunt Arizona, loves teaching. For fifteen years, she taught students in elementary school through high school. She now teaches writing and children's literature to college students in Tampa, Florida.

Gloria Houston says about her great-aunt, "She truly lives on in what she gave to her students, including me. I have traveled because she made the places in my geography book seem so real. Most important, she made each student feel special. Years later, each member of her class still thinks he or she was Aunt Arizona's pet."

Susan Condie Lamb

Susan Condie Lamb is a full-time artist who has illustrated many children's books. She has also designed sets and costumes for plays. She found that experience a big help as she drew pictures for *My Great-Aunt Arizona*.

Susan Condie Lamb grew up in Connecticut. Although she lived in New York City for a while, today she's back in Connecticut. She lives with her husband and her son, Charlie.

RESPONSE CORNER

WRITE A THANK-YOU NOTE

A Note of Thanks

Arizona Hughes was an important adult in many children's lives. Choose an important adult in your life. Write a thank-you note telling that person why he or she is special to you.

MAKE A ONE-ROOM SCHOOL

The Little Red Schoolhouse

Work with a group to turn a corner of your classroom into a model of a one-room school. Use boxes and other materials to make the desks, the stove, and other furniture. Give a tour to your classmates. Explain how this school is different from your own school.

WRITE POSTCARDS

Wish You Were Here

Suppose Great-Aunt Arizona really had traveled to faraway places. Write one or two postcards that she might have sent to her students. Share the postcards with a partner.

What Do You Think?

- What kind of person was Arizona? How do you know?

- If you could go back to Arizona's time, what would you like to see and do?

- How might Arizona's life be different if she were living today? Explain your answer.

Grandfather's Journey

**Caldecott Medal
ALA Notable Book
Teachers' Choice**

written and illustrated
by Allen Say

My grandfather was a young man when he left his home in Japan and went to see the world.

He wore European clothes for the first time and began his journey on a steamship. The Pacific Ocean astonished him.

For three weeks he did not see land. When land finally appeared it was the New World.

He explored North America by train and riverboat, and often walked for days on end.

Deserts with rocks like enormous sculptures amazed him.

The endless farm fields reminded him of the ocean he had crossed.

Huge cities of factories and tall buildings bewildered and yet excited him.

He marveled at the towering mountains and rivers as clear as the sky.

He met many people along the way. He shook hands with black men and white men, with yellow men and red men.

The more he traveled, the more he longed to see new places, and never thought of returning home.

Of all the places he visited, he liked California best. He loved the strong sunlight there, the Sierra Mountains, the lonely seacoast.

After a time, he returned to his village in Japan to marry his childhood sweetheart. Then he brought his bride to the new country.

They made their home by the San Francisco Bay and had a baby girl.

As his daughter grew, my grandfather began to think about his own childhood. He thought about his old friends.

He remembered the mountains and rivers of his home. He surrounded himself with songbirds, but he could not forget.

Finally, when his daughter was nearly grown, he could wait no more. He took his family and returned to his homeland.

Once again he saw the mountains and rivers of his childhood. They were just as he had remembered them.

Once again he exchanged stories and laughed with his old friends.

But the village was not a place for a daughter from San Francisco. So my grandfather bought a house in a large city nearby.

There, the young woman fell in love, married, and sometime later I was born.

150

When I was a small boy, my favorite weekend was a visit to my grandfather's house. He told me many stories about California.

He raised warblers and silvereyes, but he could not forget the mountains and rivers of California. So he planned a trip.

But a war began. Bombs fell from the sky and scattered our lives like leaves in a storm.

When the war ended, there was nothing left of the city and of the house where my grandparents had lived.

So they returned to the village where they had been children.
But my grandfather never kept another songbird.

The last time I saw him, my grandfather said that he longed to see California one more time. He never did.

And when I was nearly grown, I left home and went to see California for myself.

After a time, I came to love the land my grandfather had loved, and I stayed on and on until I had a daughter of my own.

But I also miss the mountains and rivers of my childhood. I miss my old friends. So I return now and then, when I can not still the longing in my heart.

The funny thing is, the moment I am in one country, I am homesick for the other.

I think I know my grandfather now.
I miss him very much.

Meet the Author and Illustrator

ALLEN SAY

Allen Say is one of America's most successful writers and illustrators of children's books. He spent two years creating *Grandfather's Journey*. After it was published in 1993, it won many of the highest honors in children's literature, including the Caldecott Medal. Allen Say's earlier books, including *El Chino, Tree of Cranes,* and *A River Dream,* have also won important awards.

Grandfather's Journey is fiction, but it is based on real life. Allen's grandfather truly was a world traveler, and he especially loved steamships. After traveling around the world, he lived in California for many years and then returned to Japan.

Allen was born in Yokohama, Japan. He began to draw even before he could walk. As a small child, Allen drew on walls, doors, and anything else he could reach. When he was twelve years old, he was thrilled to study art with a famous cartoonist in Japan.

At age sixteen, Allen Say moved to the United States. He found himself suddenly alone in a country he knew little about. He did not speak a word of English, and he felt out of place in his new school. It was a difficult time in Allen's life. He shows how he felt at that time in the painting on page 157. He says, "My favorite painting in *Grandfather's Journey* is the picture of myself, standing in the sun-drenched, empty parking lot. I love that painting."

Before Allen Say began making his living by painting, he worked as a photographer. If you look closely at the paintings in *Grandfather's Journey,* you might think they are a little like old-fashioned photographs. The people seem to be looking right at you, as if they are posing for a camera.

Allen Say has learned how to capture the feelings of his characters in his art. By sharing *Grandfather's Journey* with us, he is sharing the feelings of many immigrants to America. The next time you meet someone who has just moved to the United States, remember *Grandfather's Journey.* Remember how Allen Say must have felt as he stood in that empty parking lot.

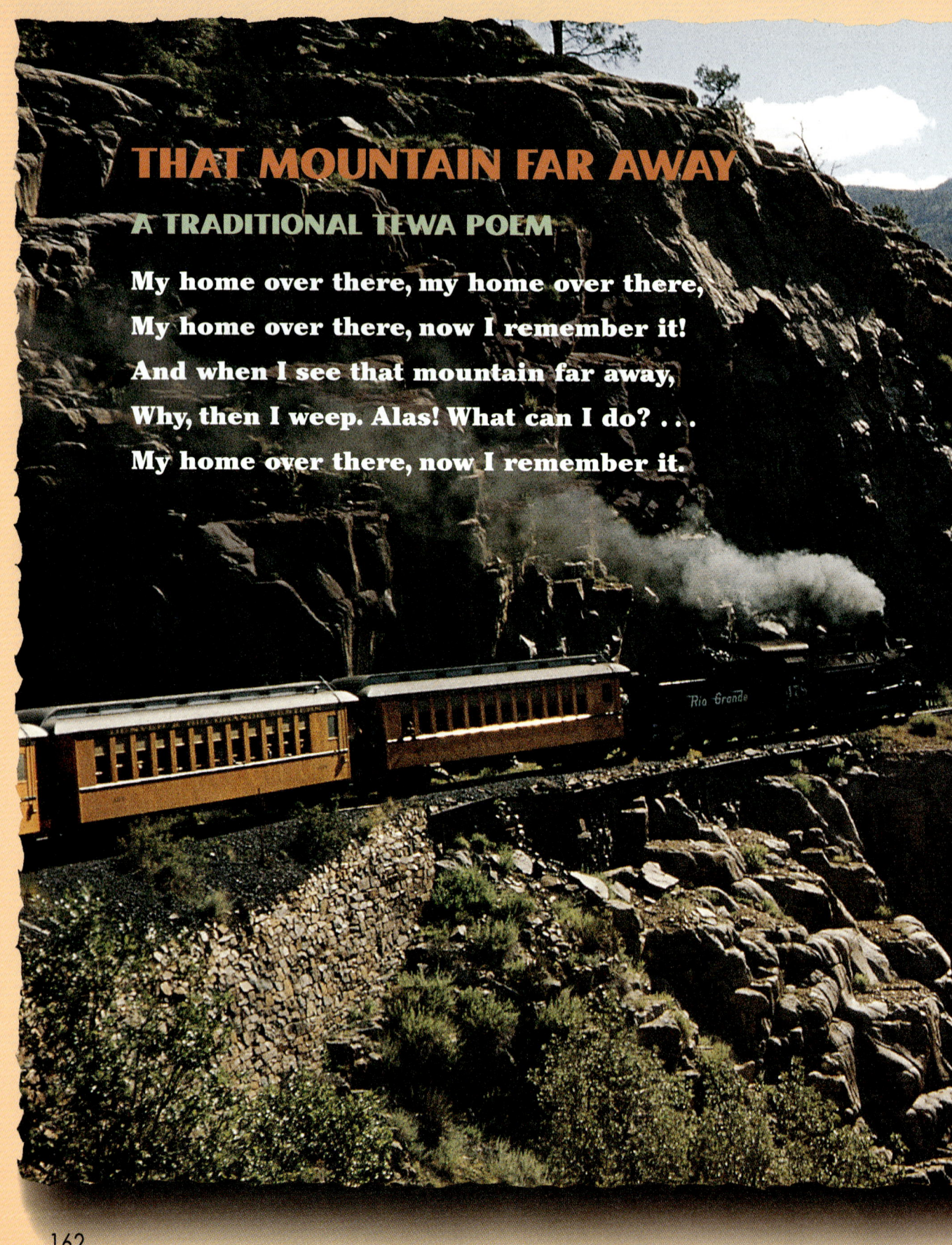

THAT MOUNTAIN FAR AWAY

A TRADITIONAL TEWA POEM

My home over there, my home over there,
My home over there, now I remember it!
And when I see that mountain far away,
Why, then I weep. Alas! What can I do? . . .
My home over there, now I remember it.

TRAVEL

EDNA ST. VINCENT MILLAY

The railroad track is miles away,
    And the day is loud with voices speaking,
Yet there isn't a train goes by all day
    But I hear its whistles shrieking.

All night there isn't a train goes by,
    Though the night is still for sleep and dreaming
But I see its cinders red on the sky
    And hear its engine steaming.

My heart is warm with the friends I make,
    And better friends I'll not be knowing,
Yet there isn't a train I wouldn't take,
    No matter where it's going.

Train from Durango to Silverton, Colorado   *Photograph by David Herman*

Response

DRAW A MAP

The Peaceful Pacific

Grandfather crossed the Pacific Ocean when he traveled from Japan to California. Look up the Pacific Ocean in an encyclopedia. Draw a map that shows the larger islands between Japan and the United States. On your map, write five interesting facts about the Pacific Ocean.

MODEL CLOTHING

What's in Style?

When he lived in America, Grandfather wore Western-style clothing. In Japan, he wore a traditional kimono. Did your ancestors wear a special kind of clothing? If you can, bring that clothing to class and model it. Or bring in a photograph that shows it. How is the special clothing different from the clothing you wear today?

Corner

MAKE A TRAVEL BROCHURE

Far, Far Away

Allen Say's grandfather and the poet who wrote "Travel" liked to visit new places. Have you seen pictures in a magazine of a place that you would like to visit? Make a travel brochure of that place. Include photographs or magazine pictures.

What Do You Think?

- How is the grandson in the story like his grandfather?

- Which of the paintings from this story is your favorite? Explain why you like it.

- Think about somewhere far away that you would like to visit someday. How would you get there? What might you see?

The Lotus Seed

by Sherry Garland
illustrated by Tatsuro Kiuchi

HOA SEN

Trong đầm gì đẹp bằng sen.
Lá xanh, bông trắng lại chen nhị vàng.
Nhị vàng, bông trắng, lá xanh,
Gần bùn mà chẳng hôi tanh mùi bùn.

—*Vô danh*

THE LOTUS FLOWER

Nothing that grows in a pond
Surpasses the beauty of the lotus flower,
With its green leaves and silky yellow styles
Amidst milky white petals.
Though mired in mud, its silky yellow styles,
Its milky white petals and green leaves
Do not smell of mud.

— Anonymous
(*translation of poem by Dinh D. Vu*)

My grandmother saw
the emperor cry
the day he lost
his golden dragon throne.

She wanted something
to remember him by,
so she snuck down
to the silent palace,
near the River of Perfumes,
and plucked a seed
from a lotus pod
that rattled
in the Imperial garden.

She hid the seed
in a special place
under the family altar,
wrapped in a piece of silk
from the *ao dai*
she wore that day.
Whenever she felt sad
or lonely,
she took out the seed
and thought of the
brave young emperor.

And when she married
a young man
chosen by her parents,
she carried the seed
inside her pocket
for good luck, long life,
and many children.
When her husband
marched off to war,
she raised her
children alone.

One day bombs fell
all around,
and soldiers
clamored door to door.
She took the time
to grab the seed,
but left her mother-of-pearl
hair combs lying
on the floor.

One terrible day
her family scrambled
into a crowded boat
and set out
on a stormy sea.
Bà watched the mountains
and the waving palms
slowly fade away.
She held the seed
in her shaking fingers
and silently said good-bye.

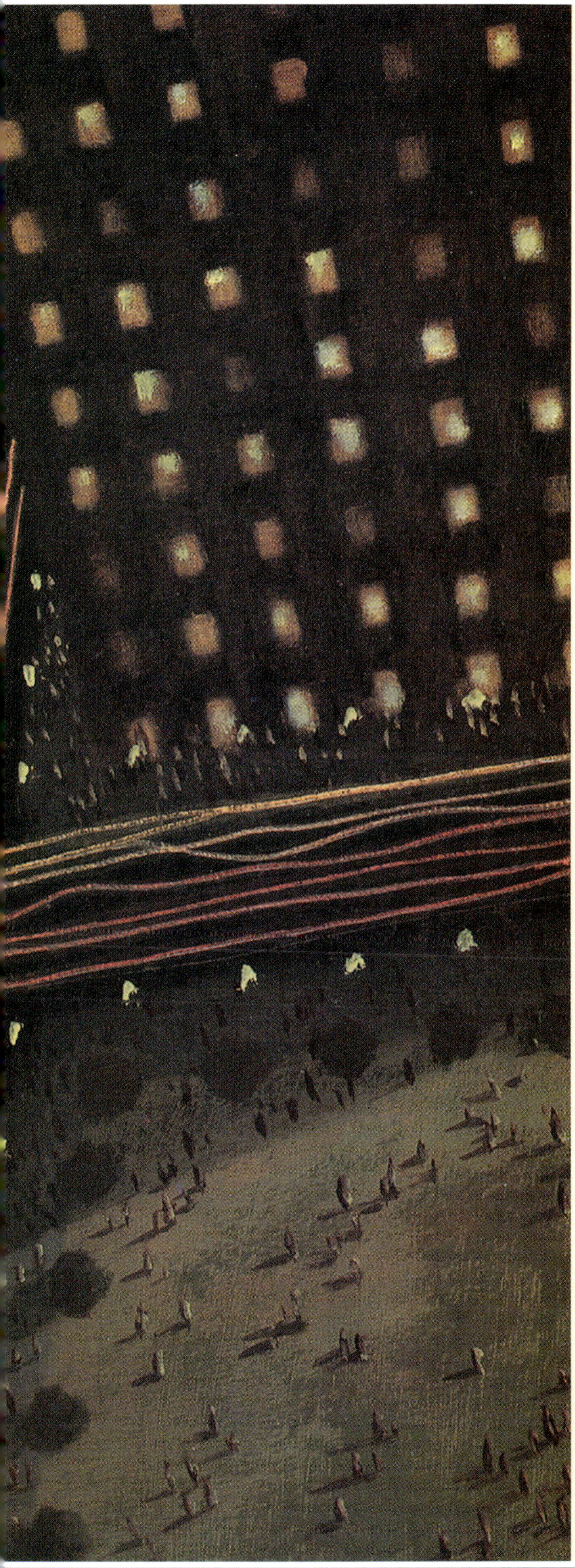

She arrived in a
strange new land
with blinking lights
and speeding cars
and towering buildings
that scraped the sky
and a language
she didn't understand.

She worked many years,
day and night,
and so did her children
and her sisters
and her cousins, too,
living together
in one big house.

Last summer
my little brother
found the special seed
and asked questions
again and again.
He'd never seen a lotus bloom
or an emperor
on a golden dragon throne.

So one night
he stole the seed
from beneath the family altar
and planted it
in a pool of mud
somewhere near Bà's
onion patch.

𝐁à cried and cried
when she found out
the seed was gone.
She didn't eat,
she didn't sleep,
and my silly brother
forgot what spot of earth
held the seed.

Then one day in spring
my grandmother shouted,
and we all ran
to the garden
and saw
a beautiful pink lotus
unfurling its petals,
so creamy and soft.

"It is the flower
of life and hope,"
my grandmother said.
"No matter how
ugly the mud
or how long the seed
lies dormant,
the bloom will
be beautiful.
It is the flower
of my country."

When the lotus blossom
faded and turned
into a pod,
Bà gave each of
her grandchildren
a seed
to remember her by,
and she kept one
for herself
to remember the emperor by.

I wrapped my seed
in a piece of silk
and hid it
in a secret place.
Someday I will plant it
and give the seeds
to my own children
and tell them about the day
my grandmother saw
the emperor cry.

Sherry Garland
Talks About The Lotus Seed

Writer Ilene Cooper interviewed Sherry Garland.

Ilene Cooper: *The Lotus Seed is about people from Vietnam. Have you ever visited that country?*

Sherry Garland: No, although I would like to very much. But I have come to know many Vietnamese people.

Cooper: *Where did the idea for The Lotus Seed come from?*

Garland: I had written a novel for adults in which a Vietnamese woman carries a lotus seed. That novel was never published. One day, the idea of the woman and her lotus seed came back to me. In one sitting, I wrote the children's book.

Cooper: *The illustrator of this book, Tatsuro Kiuchi, is Japanese. How did he do his work?*

Garland: I sent him photos of Vietnamese clothing and other things, and he worked from those. The publisher even sent him a lotus flower because he had never seen one.

Cooper: *What do Vietnamese people think of your book?*

Garland: I don't know how the people in Vietnam would feel about it. But Vietnamese Americans I have shown it to like it very much. Older people, especially those who actually came from Vietnam, remember their growing-up years fondly and talk about their country all the time.

Response Corner

PRESENT A REPORT

SYMBOLS OF AMERICA

A bald eagle, the Statue of Liberty, and the American flag are all symbols that have special meanings to Americans. Research one of these symbols. Write a short report about your choice, and present it to your classmates.

WRITE A DIARY ENTRY

TREASURES

In "The Lotus Seed," the grandmother has to leave her homeland in a hurry. She has to leave many things behind. If *you* had to leave your home quickly, what three things would you take with you? Write a diary entry explaining your choice.

WRITE A LETTER

OUR ROOTS

Sometimes young people have a hard time understanding the past. Imagine that the grandmother in the story wants to explain to her grandson what the lotus seed means to the family. Write a letter in which she tells how she felt on the day she thought the seed was lost forever. Then have her tell how she felt when the lotus flower bloomed.

What Do You Think?

- Why does the person telling this story hide her own lotus seed at the end?

- How do you think the grandmother feels when she first moves to this country? Why do you think as you do?

- People come to America from all over the world. What kinds of things do they keep to remind them of their old homes or of how their families used to live?

Art & Literature

In the 1800s, most immigrants to the United States arrived in New York by ship. Traveling across the ocean took much longer then, and the ships were not as clean and dry as modern ships. How do you think the people in this painting felt when they reached America?

Museum of the City of New York, Gift of Mrs. Robert M. Littlejohn; 8'1" x 16'6"

The Bay and Harbor of New York
by Samuel B. Waugh

Samuel B. Waugh was born in Mercer, Pennsylvania. He spent many years in Italy, but he did most of his work in Philadelphia. No one knows exactly when *The Bay and Harbor of New York* was painted, but it was probably close to 1855.

Amber Brown and Justin Daniels have been best friends since preschool. They even sit together on the imaginary trips Mr. Cohen's class takes to different parts of the world. Amber thinks her year is going great until she learns that Justin is moving to Alabama. One day while Justin is packing a box of important items, the two friends get into an argument about keeping a chewing gum ball that they have been adding to for a year and a half. Will they make up?

Today, Mr. Cohen's class is going to have a pizza party.

That's the good news.

The bad news is that it's a going-away party for my ex-best friend, Justin Daniels, and we still haven't spoken to each other.

I've been waiting for him to say "I'm sorry."

I don't know what he's been waiting for.

So we've been sitting in class right next to each other without saying a word.

Well, hardly a word.

I confess. Once I did say, "Hey, dirt bag. Would you please pass the eraser?"

And he said, "Crayon brain, get your own eraser."

It hurts a lot but I'm not going to give in on this one.

Justin is just so stubborn.

Today, the class "returned" from our trip to China. Next we'll be "going" to Australia.

I can't wait.

Justin, however, won't be "going." He'll be going to Alabama for real.

I wish Al Abama was a real person so I could tell him how much I hate him.

As Brandi Colwin walks by our desks, I call out, "Hey, Brandi. Don't forget. We're going to sit next to each other when we go to Australia."

Then Justin turns to Hannah and says, "I'll be sure to send you some postcards from Alabama."

I yawn, a big yawn, right in his face, to show I don't care, and then I pretend to scrunch up over my worksheet so that he can't see that I'm very close to crying.

Mr. Cohen flicks the lights off and on.

"The pizza will be here in five minutes. Extra cheese, mushrooms, the works."

I pick up my head and look over at Justin. He doesn't look any happier than I feel.

I make a decision and call out, "Tell the guy to hold the anchovies," and then look right at Justin, pretending to be holding wiggly anchovies.

He starts to laugh.

I pretend to flip an anchovy over to him.

He pretends to grab it.

"Let's go stand in the hall for a minute," Justin says, picking up his knapsack.

We both walk over to Mr. Cohen and ask to go out in the hall for a few minutes.

"Sure." He motions to the door.

As we walk out, I think I hear Mr. Cohen say, "Finally."

Once we get out there, we just stand quietly for a few minutes.

Then we both say "I'm sorry" at the same time and link pinkies.

"I don't want you to go." I start to cry, just a little.

Justin takes a deep breath and says, "I don't want to go either. You think this is easy? My new school is so big. I don't know anyone there. What if I forget my locker combination? All the kids there already know each other. My parents say I have to be brave, to be a good example for Danny. That it will be fun. But I know my mom is nervous about moving, too. I heard her talking to your mom. And it's too late to join a little league team, and everyone there thinks I talk funny and I have to learn to say 'Y'all' and 'Ma'am,' and . . . and . . ."

I say, "And?"

Justin turns red. "And I'm going to miss you."

I smile for what seems like the first time in years.

We stand for a few minutes and then I say, "Why didn't you tell me that sooner?"

"Because you stopped talking to me," he says.

"You wouldn't talk to me." I defend myself. "Not about the important stuff."

"It's hard." He looks down at his untied shoelaces.

I say, "I want you to stay."

Justin looks up. "Me, too. But I can't. My parents are making me go. But they said you and your mom could visit this summer."

This summer. I better start practicing "Y'all" and "Ma'am."

Justin pulls something out of his knapsack.

It's a badly wrapped present.

I open the package.

It's a tissue box.

Inside the tissue box is the chewing gum ball.

"Thanks. It's the best present ever," I say, knowing that I will save it for the rest of my life.

The pizza guy arrives with ten pizzas. My stomach smells the extra cheese. Mr. Cohen comes out.

"You two better get inside before everyone eats up all of this pizza. It's your party, Justin."

As we walk inside, I think about how it will be when Justin and I grow up and he doesn't have to move just because his parents move.

Maybe someday we can open our own company. I'll be president one week and he'll be president the next. We'll sell jars of icing and boxes of cookies.

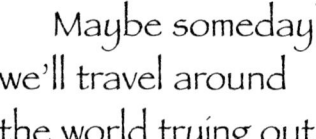

Maybe someday we'll travel around the world trying out new flavors of chewing gum, and the chewing gum ball will get so big that we'll build a house for it.

Until then, maybe, I can save some of my allowance each week and call Justin once in a while. He can do the same.

I think I'm going to learn his new phone number by heart.

Whenever I think about third grade, I'm going to think about Justin, and I bet he's always going to think about me.

SAY HELLO TO Paula Danziger

Paula Danziger knew in the second grade that she wanted to be a writer. That's when she began noticing and remembering things that happened to her so she could write about them later.

During Paula's childhood, her family moved a lot. She lived in Washington, D.C., in New Jersey, and in a rented farmhouse in Pennsylvania. Paula read books all the time. "Thank goodness for the local librarian. She gave me lots of wonderful books to read, and she let me know she cared."

Paula Danziger was once a teacher, and she uses her teaching experiences in her writing. Some of the events in her books come from real things that happened in her classroom. "What matters to me is that kids like my books, and that my books touch their lives and make them feel less alone."

READ A MAP
Map It Out

Amber will have a friend in another part of the country. On a map, find the places where your family and friends live. In what direction would you travel to get to their homes? About how far would you have to travel? Use the distance scale and the compass rose to help you. Share your findings with your family and classmates.

WRITE AN ADVICE COLUMN
Make Up and Be Friends

Friends sometimes have disagreements. With a partner, talk about why friends might disagree and how they can make up. Write an advice column about disagreements. Take turns writing and answering the questions. Share your "column" with your class.

TELL JOKES

Joking Around

A sense of humor can help you make and keep friends. It worked for Amber! Look through some joke books to find jokes that you think others might enjoy. Read a few of them to your class.

What Do You Think?

- What problem must Amber Brown face?

- Would you like to read more about Amber Brown? Why or why not?

- Justin is nervous about moving. How do you think he will feel about his new home a year from now? Why do you think so?

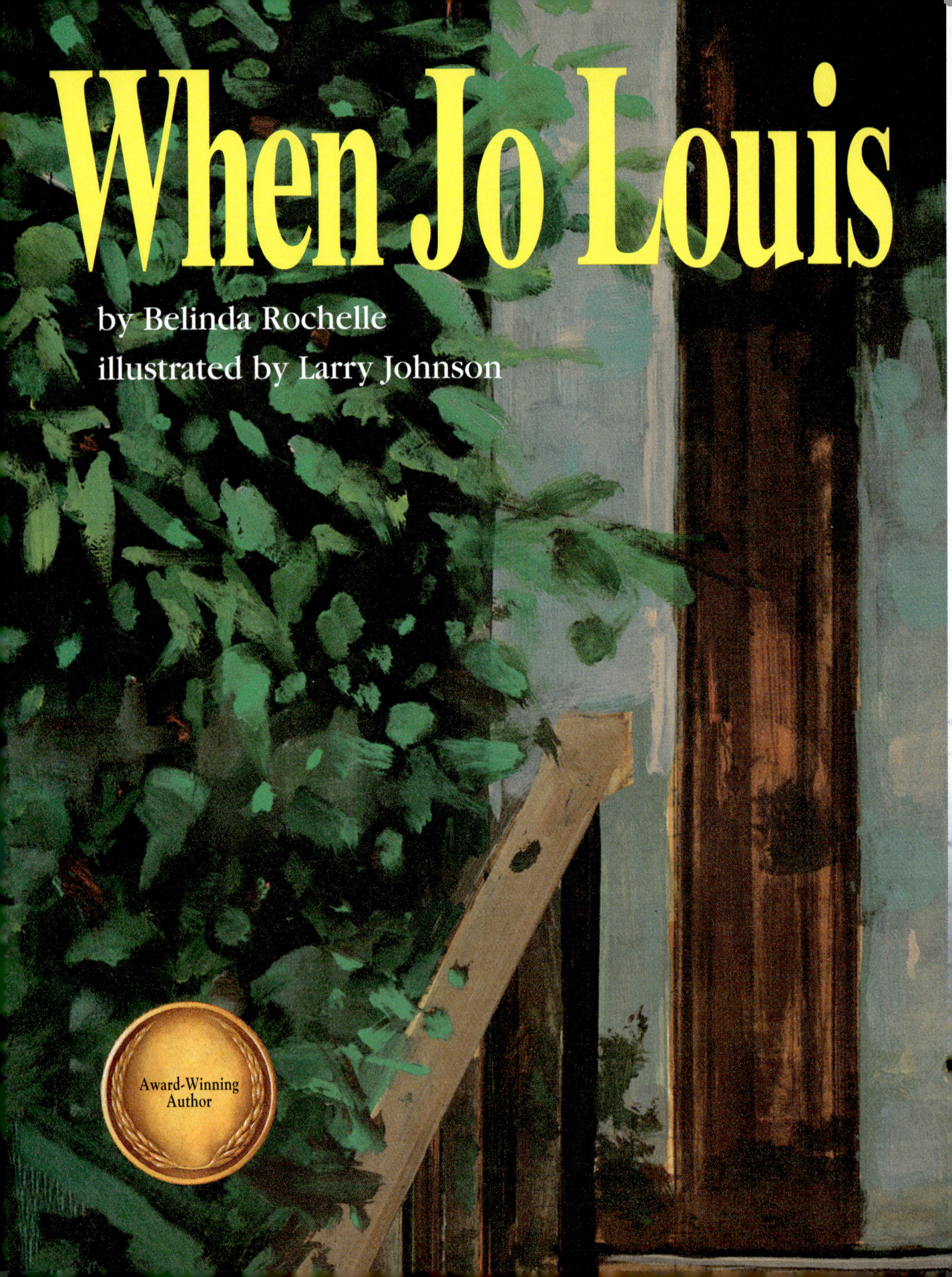

When Jo Louis

by Belinda Rochelle
illustrated by Larry Johnson

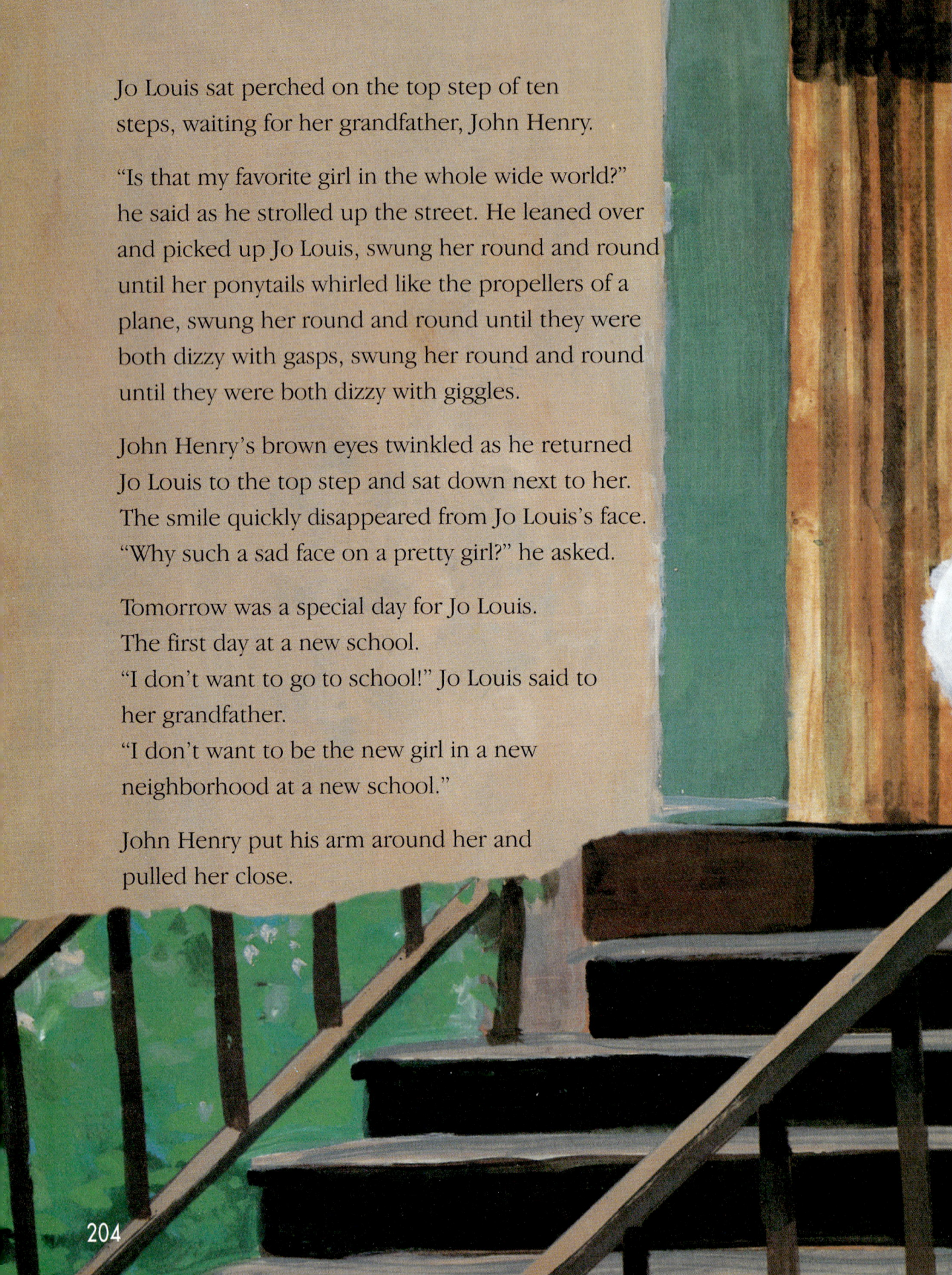

Jo Louis sat perched on the top step of ten steps, waiting for her grandfather, John Henry.

"Is that my favorite girl in the whole wide world?" he said as he strolled up the street. He leaned over and picked up Jo Louis, swung her round and round until her ponytails whirled like the propellers of a plane, swung her round and round until they were both dizzy with gasps, swung her round and round until they were both dizzy with giggles.

John Henry's brown eyes twinkled as he returned Jo Louis to the top step and sat down next to her. The smile quickly disappeared from Jo Louis's face. "Why such a sad face on a pretty girl?" he asked.

Tomorrow was a special day for Jo Louis.
The first day at a new school.
"I don't want to go to school!" Jo Louis said to her grandfather.
"I don't want to be the new girl in a new neighborhood at a new school."

John Henry put his arm around her and pulled her close.

"Why don't you want to go to school?" he asked.

"I'll probably be the shortest kid in class, or I'll be the one who can't run as fast as the other kids. I finish every race last."

"It's just a matter of time before a new school is an old school. Just a matter of time before you'll be able to run really fast, and you won't always finish last," he said, patting her hand.
"What's the real reason you don't want to go to school?" John Henry asked.

Jo Louis shook her head. It was hard to explain. She just knew it would happen. Someone would ask THE question. IT was THE question, the same question each and every time she met someone new:
"What's your name?"
It was that moment, that question, that made Jo Louis want to disappear. And it really wouldn't make a difference if she were taller, and it wouldn't make a difference that she was the new kid in school, and it wouldn't make a difference if she could run really fast. She just wished that she didn't have to tell anyone her name.

Her grandfather picked her up and placed her on his knee. "Let me tell you a story," he said.

"When I was just a young boy living in Mississippi," he began, "I used to dream about moving north. To me it was the promised land. I wanted to find a good job in the big city. Cities like Chicago, St. Louis. But everybody, I mean everybody, talked about Harlem in New York City. Going north, it was all anybody ever talked about. I would sit on the front porch and just daydream about those big-city places. The way some folks told it everything was perfect. Even the streets in the big city were paved with gold, and it was all there just waiting for me." John Henry's eyes sparkled as his voice quickened. "When I saved enough money, I crowded onto the train with other small-town folks headed north. Everything I owned fit into a torn, tattered suitcase and a brown box wrapped in string.

"I rode the train all day and all night. Like a snake winding its way across the Mississippi River, that train moved slowly through farmlands and flatland, over mountains and valleys, until it reached its final destination."

Jo Louis closed her eyes.
She loved her grandfather's stories—his words were like wings and other things. She listened closely until she felt she was right there with him.

"'New York City! New York! New York!' the conductor bellowed as the train pulled into the station.

"I headed straight to Harlem. I had never seen buildings so tall. They almost seemed to touch the sky. Even the moon looked different in the big city. The moonlight was bright and shining, the stars skipped across the sky.

"The streets sparkled in the night sky's light. It was true! The streets did seem to be paved in gold! I walked up and down city streets that stretched wide and long. I walked past a fancy nightclub, where you could hear the moaning of a saxophone and a woman singing so sad, so soft, and so slow that the music made me long for home.

"And then, all of a sudden the sad music changed to happy music. That saxophone and singing started to swing. Hundreds of people spilled out into the sidewalks, waving flags, scarves, waving handkerchiefs and tablecloths. Hundreds of people filled the streets with noise and laughter, waving hats and anything and everything, filling the sky with bright colors of red, white, green, yellow, blue, purple, and orange.

"Everybody was clapping, hands were raised high to the sky. Up and down the street, people were shouting and singing. Cars were beeping their horns; bells were ringing.

'Excuse me.' I patted a woman on the shoulder.
'What's going on?' I asked.
The woman smiled.
She was pretty with soft, brown hair
and a friendly smile.
'Why, haven't you heard?' she said,
'Joe Louis won the title fight.
My name is Mary'—she held out
her hand—'and your name is…?'"

John Henry smiled and hugged Jo Louis close.
"It was a special night for me. It was a special night for black people everywhere.
Joe Louis was the greatest boxer in the world. He was a hero. That night he won the fight of his life. A fight that a lot of people thought he would lose. Some folks said he was too slow, others said he wasn't strong enough.
But he worked hard and won. It was a special night, my first night in the big city, and Joe Louis won the fight. But the night was special for another reason."

"It was the night you met Grandma," Jo Louis said, and she started to smile.

"It was a special night that I'll never forget. I named your father Joe Louis, and he named you, his first child, Jo Louis, too."
Her grandfather tickled her nose.
"That was the night you won the title. You should be very proud of your name. Every name has a special story."

The next day Jo Louis took a deep breath as she walked into her new school classroom and slipped into a seat.
The boy sitting next to Jo Louis tapped her on the shoulder. "My name is Lester. What's your name?"

Jo answered slowly, "My name is Jo . . . Jo Louis."
She balled her fist and closed her eyes and braced herself.
She waited, waited for the laughter, waited for the jokes.
She peeked out of one eye, then she peeked out the other eye.

"Wow, what a great name!" he said, and smiled.

Author Belinda Rochelle

Belinda Rochelle loves sports. "I remember my grandmother telling me stories about Joe Louis," she says, "and about what his fights meant to African Americans." Years later, Belinda Rochelle used her grandmother's stories to help her write *When Jo Louis Won the Title*.

Belinda Rochelle's first writing project was about another famous American—Abraham Lincoln. When she was in sixth grade, she wrote a play for her class about President Lincoln. That's when Belinda knew that she wanted to become a writer.

Illustrator Larry Johnson

When Larry Johnson was in third grade, he learned two important things about himself. The first was that he loved sports. The second was that he had a talent for art. So he began making drawings about sports and sports figures.

When Jo Louis Won the Title isn't really a sports story, but Larry Johnson's love of sports made him a "natural" to illustrate it. The fact that he is a grandfather made the job even more fun for him!

Response Corner

MAKE A POSTER

Being the New Kid

How would you feel if you were Jo Louis, in a new neighborhood and a new school? Work with a group to make a poster for new students like Jo Louis. Write ten tips that could help a new student feel at home in your school.

RETELL A FOLKTALE

Legends of the Past

Jo Louis's grandfather was named for John Henry, an African American folk hero. Read the folktale about John Henry, and find a copy of the song about him. Retell the tale to your classmates. If you like to sing, perform the song as well.

DRAW PICTURES

Harlem Heroes

Jo's grandfather was raised in Mississippi, but he traveled to Harlem in New York City. Many other African Americans traveled to Harlem at the same time. Look up Harlem in an encyclopedia. Start a picture gallery of famous African Americans who have lived in this community. Draw their faces, and add information about why they are important.

What Do You Think?

- How does her grandfather's story make Jo Louis feel?

- Jo Louis was worried that she would be teased about her name. Why is it wrong for children to tease each other about their names?

- How did the people in New York City feel about the fighter Joe Louis? Is there a sports star who is important to your community? Why is that person important?

Theme Wrap-Up

Why do you think some people want to travel to new places? Why do some people prefer to stay home? Think about the characters in this theme to help you answer.

If Great-Aunt Arizona met Jo Louis, what do you think they would say to each other? Why do you think so?

ACTIVITY CORNER

Find out about newcomers in your town or city, or in a city nearby. First, call or write to the Chamber of Commerce. Ask how many people have moved to the area in the past five years. Then, find out where most of the newcomers came from. Share your results with your classmates.

Glossary

WHAT IS A GLOSSARY?

A glossary is like a small dictionary at the back of a book. It lists some of the words used in the book, along with their pronunciations, their meanings, and other useful information. If you come across a word you don't know as you are reading, you can look up the word in this glossary.

Using the

Like a dictionary, this glossary lists words in alphabetical order. To find a word, look it up by its first letter or letters.

To save time, use the **guide words** at the top of each page. These show you the first and last words on the page. Look at the guide words to see if your word falls between them alphabetically.

Here is an example of a glossary entry:

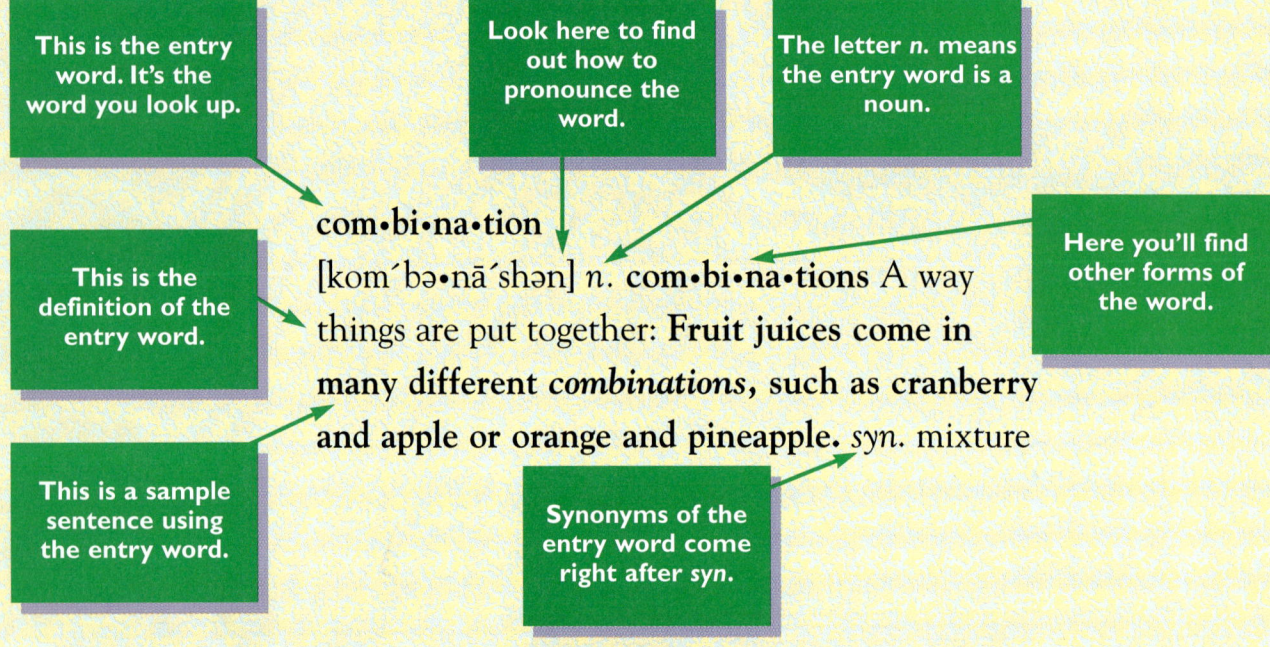

ETYMOLOGY

Etymology is the study or history of how words are developed. Words often have interesting backgrounds that can help you remember what they mean. Look in the margins of the glossary to find the etymologies of certain words.

Here is an example of an etymology:

value   The Latin word *valēre* means "to be strong." The Old French language used this word to make the word *value*, changing the meaning to "worth."

Glossary

PRONUNCIATION

The pronunciation in brackets is a respelling that shows how the word is pronounced.

The **pronunciation key** explains what the symbols in a respelling mean. A shortened pronunciation key appears on every other page of the glossary.

PRONUNCIATION KEY*

a	add, map	m	move, seem	u	up, done
ā	ace, rate	n	nice, tin	û(r)	burn, term
â(r)	care, air	ng	ring, song	yōō	fuse, few
ä	palm, father	o	odd, hot	v	vain, eve
b	bat, rub	ō	open, so	w	win, away
ch	check, catch	ô	order, jaw	y	yet, yearn
d	dog, rod	oi	oil, boy	z	zest, muse
e	end, pet	ou	pout, now	zh	vision, pleasure
ē	equal, tree	ŏŏ	took, full	ə	the schwa, an unstressed vowel representing the sound spelled
f	fit, half	ōō	pool, food		
g	go, log	p	pit, stop		
h	hope, hate	r	run, poor		
i	it, give	s	see, pass		*a* in *above*
ī	ice, write	sh	sure, rush		*e* in *sicken*
j	joy, ledge	t	talk, sit		*i* in *possible*
k	cool, take	th	thin, both		*o* in *melon*
l	look, rule	t̸h	this, bathe		*u* in *circus*

Other symbols:
- • separates words into syllables
- ´ indicates heavier stress on a syllable
- ` indicates light stress on a syllable

Abbreviations: *adj.* adjective, *adv.* adverb, *conj.* conjunction, *interj.* interjection, *n.* noun, *prep.* preposition, *pron.* pronoun, *syn.* synonym, *v.* verb.

*The Pronunciation Key, adapted entries, and the Short Key that appear on the following pages are reprinted from *HBJ School Dictionary* Copyright © 1990 by Harcourt Brace & Company. Reprinted by permission of Harcourt Brace & Company.

affect

amount
Amount comes from the Latin word meaning "to the mountain" or "upward." An *amount* may be the total number when counting upward or adding.

af·fect
[ə·fekt´] *v.* **af·fects** To change; to cause something else to happen: **This experiment shows how sunlight *affects* the growth of plants.** *syn.* influence

al·low·ance
[ə·lou´əns] *n.* A set sum of money a person gets regularly, such as each week: **Gordon gets an *allowance* of five dollars every week.**

a·mount
[ə·mount´] *n.* A certain number of something; a sum: **The *amount* of money I had was not enough to buy the poster.** *syn.* quantity

anx·ious
[angk´shəs] *adj.* Worried; uneasy: **Valerie was *anxious* about oversleeping because she thought she might miss the school bus.**

ar·rive
[ə·rīv´] *v.* **ar·rived** To get to a place: **Ivan *arrived* at the game at four o'clock.** *syn.* reach

as·ton·ish
[ə·ston´ish] *v.* **as·ton·ished** To surprise; to fill with wonder: **It was a clear night, and the number of stars in the sky *astonished* him.** *syn.* amaze

blind
[blīnd] *adj.* Unable to see: **Bats are nearly *blind*, so they use sound to tell them which way to fly.**

brace
[brās] *v.* **braced** To prepare for something that might be bad; to hold oneself tightly in place: **Ryan held onto a pole on the bus as he *braced* himself for a sudden stop.**

buck•et
[buk´it] *n.* **buck•ets** A round container with a flat bottom and a curved handle, used to carry things: **Shelly filled two *buckets* with water, got some soap and a mop, and was ready to wash the floor.** *syn.* pail

C

cab•in

[kab´in] *n.* A small wooden house, sometimes made of big logs: **Our family stays in a *cabin* by a lake every summer.** *syn.* hut

car•pen•ter
[kär´pən•tər] *n.* A person who makes things out of wood: **The *carpenter* made a bookcase for our room.**

child•hood
[chīld´hood´] *n.* The time when someone is young: **Tara had a very happy *childhood* and always played with her friends.** *syn.* youth

choice
[chois] *n.* **choic•es** The act of picking which one: **There were many *choices* to make at the bakery, but we decided to get muffins and apple tarts.** *syns.* decision, selection

choice

bucket The Old English word *buc* also means "belly." A *bucket* is a container that holds things, just as a belly is a container that holds food.

cabin

a	add	oo	took
ā	ace	ōō	pool
â	care	u	up
ä	palm	û	burn
e	end	yōō	fuse
ē	equal	oi	oil
i	it	ou	pout
ī	ice	ng	ring
o	odd	th	thin
ō	open	th	this
ô	order	zh	vision

ə = { *a* in *above*
e in *sicken*
i in *possible*
o in *melon*
u in *circus* }

combination

comfortable
This word comes from *comfort,* which used to mean "strong." In the 1800s, its meaning changed and became "at ease."

creek

com·bi·na·tion [kom´bə·nā´shən] *n.* **com·bi·na·tions** A way things are put together: **Fruit juices come in many different *combinations,* such as cranberry and apple or orange and pineapple.** *syn.* mixture

com·fort·a·ble [kum´fər·tə·bəl] *adj.* Restful; at ease: **In the summer, José feels *comfortable* in his air-conditioned house.**

com·mer·cial [kə·mûr´shəl] *n.* An advertisement on television or radio, used for selling something: **The *commercial* for the new cereal made Kelly feel hungry.**

con·grat·u·la·tions [kən·grach´ə·lā´shənz] *n.* Good wishes letting someone know you are happy for him or her: ***Congratulations* on your team's great game!**

crea·ture [krē´chər] *n.* **crea·tures** An animal: **Many different *creatures* live in the rain forest.**

creek [krēk or krik] *n.* A small, narrow river that may not be very deep: **The cowboy got fresh water for his horse from the *creek*.** *syn.* stream

cu·ri·ous [kyoor´ē·əs] *adj.* Wanting to know or find out more: **Elena was *curious* and wanted to learn how rainbows are formed.** *syn.* questioning

depth
[depth] *n.* **depths** A far distance into something; the part deep down: **The sunken ship was lost in the *depths* of the sea.**

des•ti•na•tion
[des´tə•nā´shən] *n.* The place someone is going to; a goal: **The *destination* of our trip was New York City, and we were eager to get there.**

de•stroy
[di•stroi´] *v.* **de•stroyed** To put an end to; to break something apart so badly that it cannot be fixed: **After the storm, our garden was *destroyed* and we had to replant everything.** *syns.* ruin, wreck

dor•mant
[dôr´mənt] *adj.* Not moving or growing for a period of time; at rest: **The plants under the snow are *dormant*, but they will grow again in the spring.** *syn.* asleep

earn
[ûrn] *v.* **earned** To get as payment for hard work: **Han *earned* some money by washing cars.** *syn.* gain

ech•o
[ek´ō] *n.* **ech•oes** A sound that comes back again: **Tommy shouted into the cave and heard the *echoes* of his voice come back softer and softer, again and again.** *syn.* repetition

echo

depths *Depth* comes from the word *deep*. *Deep* comes from a word that means "diving duck." Many words have come from *deep*, such as *dimple*, *dip*, and *dive*.

earn

a	add	o͝o	took
ā	ace	o͞o	pool
â	care	u	up
ä	palm	û	burn
e	end	yo͞o	fuse
ē	equal	oi	oil
i	it	ou	pout
ī	ice	ng	ring
o	odd	th	thin
ō	open	t̸h	this
ô	order	zh	vision

ə = { *a* in *above*, *e* in *sicken*, *i* in *possible*, *o* in *melon*, *u* in *circus* }

339

emperor

graze

hesitate
Hesitate once meant "to become stuck." It now means "to pause or wait."

em·per·or
[em´pər·ər] *n.* A person who rules a land: The *emperor* lived in a beautiful palace, and he made all the laws himself. *syn.* king

en·er·gy
[en´ər·jē] *n.* The force or power to make things work; the ability to make things go: Eating breakfast in the morning gives me *energy* to work during the day.

ex·ist
[ig·zist´] *v.* To be; to live: Dinosaurs do not *exist* anymore, but we can learn about them in books.

ex·tinc·tion
[ik·stingk´shən] *n.* When there is no more of a kind of animal or plant: The white tigers in India are faced with *extinction* because people have hunted them too much.

graze
[grāz] *v.* **graz·ing** To feed on grass: The cows were *grazing* on the hillside where the grass was thick.

hes·i·tate
[hez´ə·tāt´] *v.* To stop and think whether to do or say something: Carol saw her father *hesitate* before he bought the purple lamp. *syns.* pause, delay

home·sick
[hōm´sik´] *adj.* Sad because you miss your family and the place you live: Aretha was very *homesick* while she was at overnight camp. *syn.* lonely

I

i·den·ti·fy
[ī·den′tə·fī′] *v.*
i·den·ti·fied To see and know by name; to point out: Julian *identified* three butterflies while on a field trip to the park. *syn.* recognize

im·age
[im′ij] *n.* A picture or likeness of, as seen in a mirror: Katy saw her *image* reflected in the store window. *syn.* appearance

im·pa·tience
[im·pā′shəns] *n.* A feeling of not wanting to wait; not wanting things to slow down: Sam made a mistake on the test because of his *impatience* to be the first one done. *syn.* eagerness

L

ledge
[lej] *n.* A narrow, flat shelf that sticks out from a steep rock or wall: Carlos put some flowerpots on the *ledge* outside the window.

M

man·ners
[man′ərz] *n.* Polite ways to do things; ways to do things that show good behavior: My mother taught me the good *manners* to always say "Please" and "Thank you." *syn.* etiquette

mol·ten
[mōl′tən] *adj.* Made into a hot liquid by heat: When a volcano becomes active, *molten* rock, or lava, flows out of it.

molten

ledge

molten *Molten* is from the word *melt*. The first meaning of *melt* was "soft." When something *melts*, it usually becomes a liquid or a "soft" substance.

a	add	o͝o	took
ā	ace	o͞o	pool
â	care	u	up
ä	palm	û	burn
e	end	yo͞o	fuse
ē	equal	oi	oil
i	it	ou	pout
ī	ice	ng	ring
o	odd	th	thin
ō	open	th	this
ô	order	zh	vision

ə = { *a* in *above*
        e in *sicken*
        i in *possible*
        o in *melon*
        u in *circus* }

341

nervous

peculiar
Peculiar comes from a Latin word meaning "private property." **Pecu** means "cattle," and years ago cattle were very important property. The meaning then changed to "belonging only to oneself." In English, it came to mean "being the only one of its kind."

ner•vous
[nûr´vəs] *adj.* Worried and somewhat fearful: **I felt *nervous* about singing in front of the class, but I did it anyway.** *syn.* uneasy

or•bit
[ôr´bit] *v.* **orbits** To move around another object, usually in space: **The Earth *orbits* the sun once a year.** *syn.* circle

pave
[pāv] *v.* **paved** To cover an area of ground with something hard, such as concrete: **The street in front of my house was once dirt, but it was *paved* last week.**

pe•cul•iar
[pi•kyōōl´yər] *adj.* Belonging to only one person or thing; strange or unusual: **Jennifer had a *peculiar* dog that ate carrots.** *syns.* unique, odd

peer
[pir] *v.* **peer•ing** To look closer to see more clearly: **Billy was *peering* under the bed, looking for his shoes.**

pop•u•la•tion
[pop´yə•lā´shən] *n.* **pop•u•la•tions** A group or kind; a certain group of people or animals living in one place: Some owl *populations* are in danger because people are cutting down too many of the trees that they live in. *syn.* inhabitants

post•card
[pōst´kärd´] *n.* **post•cards** A stiff, rectangular piece of paper with a picture on one side and writing space on the other side, made to be sent through the mail: While Carmen was traveling with her parents, she kept in touch with her friends by sending them *postcards*.

re•ceive
[ri•sēv´] *v.* To get something, as in a gift: I will *receive* 5 cents for every soda can I turn in. *syns.* acquire, obtain

re•mind
[ri•mīnd´] *v.* **re•mind•ed** To cause to remember; to make someone think of something again: The tacos *reminded* Jane of her trip to Mexico and of the wonderful food she ate there.

sax•o•phone
[sak´sə•fōn´] *n.* A musical instrument in the shape of a curved brass tube: Mike plays a *saxophone* in the band.

saxophone

saxophone

a	add	o͝o	took
ā	ace	o͞o	pool
â	care	u	up
ä	palm	û	burn
e	end	yo͞o	fuse
ē	equal	oi	oil
i	it	ou	pout
ī	ice	ng	ring
o	odd	th	thin
ō	open	t̸h	this
ô	order	zh	vision

ə = { *a* in *above*, *e* in *sicken*, *i* in *possible*, *o* in *melon*, *u* in *circus* }

343

seacoast

soldier The Latin word *solidus* means "military pay." French changed it to *solde*, and the person getting the military pay was called a *soldior*. English changed it to *soldier*.

soldier

sea·coast
[sē´kōst´] *n.* The area where the land meets the ocean: **When walking along the *seacoast*, it is fun to watch the waves.** *syns.* shore, beach

silk
[silk] *n.* A kind of cloth made from a strong, shiny, threadlike material: **Suki likes scarves made of *silk* because they feel so smooth.**

sol·dier
[sōl´jər] *n.* **sol·diers** A person in the army; someone who watches over others and keeps them from harm: **The *soldiers* guard the queen when she is outside the palace.** *syns.* protector, fighter

spy
[spī] *v.* To watch closely without being seen: **The little kids always *spy* on us because they want to find our secret clubhouse.**

sur·face
[sûr´fis] *n.* The outer part of something; the outer layer that covers something: **The *surface* of the moon is rocky and dry.**

sur·vive
[sər·vīv´] *v.* To live through; to stay alive: **Dolphins need to come up for air in order to *survive* in the ocean.** *syn.* remain

swal·low
[swol´ō] *v.* To make something go down the throat and into the stomach: **I try to chew my food well, so it will be easy to *swallow*.**

tame
[tām] *adj.* Under control, not wild: The **tame** animals in the petting zoo will not bite.
syn. gentle

throne
[thrōn] *n.* A chair for a ruler: The king sat on his **throne** as the crown was placed on his head.

un·der·ground
[un´dər·ground´] *adj.* Below the earth: We went into the tunnel and rode the **underground** train.

uni·verse
[yōō´nə·vûrs´] *n.* Everything in the world; the sun, stars, and planets: Astronauts see parts of the **universe** that cannot be seen from Earth.

val·ue
[val´yōō] *n.* The worth; the price: This painting has great **value** because the painter is famous.
syn. cost

view
[vyōō] *n.* What can be seen from a place: I have a **view** of the street from my window.

yawn
[yôn] *v.* To open the mouth wide when one is sleepy: Tyrone was sleepy and he soon began to **yawn**.

yawn

throne

value The Latin word *valēre* means "to be strong." The Old French language used this word to make the word *value*, changing the meaning to "worth."

a	add	ŏŏ	took
ā	ace	ōō	pool
â	care	u	up
ä	palm	û	burn
e	end	yōō	fuse
ē	equal	oi	oil
i	it	ou	pout
ī	ice	ng	ring
o	odd	th	thin
ō	open	t̶h̶	this
ô	order	zh	vision

ə = { a in *above*, e in *sicken*, i in *possible*, o in *melon*, u in *circus* }

INDEX OF Titles and Authors

Page numbers in color refer to biographical information.

Aardema, Verna, **18**, *34*

All Eyes on the Pond, **84**

Amber Brown Is Not a Crayon, **190**

Borreguita and the Coyote, **18**

Bug Sat in a Silver Flower, A, **80**

Carrison, Muriel Paskin, **314**

Class Act, A, **272**

Cleary, Beverly, **316**, *329*

Creative Minds at Work, **266**

Danziger, Paula, **190**, *199*

Garland, Sherry, **166**, *185*

Gibbons, Gail, **38**, *49*

Godkin, Celia, **54**

Grandfather's Journey, **130**

Houston, Gloria, **114**, *127*

Hubbell, Patricia, **258**

I Am Flying!, **256**

If You Made a Million, **278**

Inventor Thinks Up Helicopters, The, **258**

Journey Through the Solar System, **226**

King and the Poor Boy, The, **314**

Kuskin, Karla, **80**

Lotus Seed, The, **166**

Marzollo, Jean, **266**

Millay, Edna St. Vincent, **163**

My Great-Aunt Arizona, **114**

Nature's Great Balancing Act, **64**

Norsgaard, E. Jaediker, **64**

Patently Ridiculous, **262**

Prelutsky, Jack, **256**

Prince, Saul T., **262**

Ramona and Her Father, **316**

Rochelle, Belinda, **202**, 217

Rosen, Michael J., **84**, 105

Say, Allen, **130**, 160

Schwartz, David M., **278**, 310

Stannard, Russell, **226**

That Mountain Far Away, **162**

Travel, **163**

When Jo Louis Won the Title, **202**

Wolf Island, **54**

Wolves, **38**

Copyright © 1997 by Harcourt Brace & Company

All rights reserved. No part of this publication may be reproduced or transmitted in any form or by any means, electronic or mechanical, including photocopy, recording, or any information storage and retrieval system, without permission in writing from the publisher.

Requests for permission to make copies of any part of the work should be mailed to: Permissions Department, Harcourt Brace & Company, 6277 Sea Harbor Drive, Orlando, Florida 32887-6777.

HARCOURT BRACE and Quill Design is a registered trademark of Harcourt Brace & Company.

Printed in the United States of America

Acknowledgments

For permission to reprint copyrighted material, grateful acknowledgment is made to the following sources:

Beautiful America Publishing Company: Cover illustration by Carol Johnson from *A Journey of Hope/Una Jornada de Esperanza* by Bob Harvey and Diane Kelsay Harvey. Copyright 1991 by Little America Publishing Co.

Curtis Brown Ltd.: Corrected galley from *Borreguita and the Coyote* by Verna Aardema. Originally published in *A Bookworm Who Hatched*, Richard C. Owen Publishers, Inc., 1993.

Children's Television Workshop: "Patently Ridiculous" by Saul T. Prince, illustrated by John Lawrence/Bernstein & Associates from *3-2-1 Contact* Magazine, May 1994. Copyright 1994 by Children's Television Workshop. "A Class Act" from *Kid City* Magazine, March 1993. Text copyright 1993 by Children's Television Workshop.

Dial Books for Young Readers, a division of Penguin Books USA Inc.: Cover illustration by Jerry Pinkney from *Back Home* by Gloria Jean Pinkney. Illustration copyright © 1992 by Jerry Pinkney.

Dutton Signet, a division of Penguin Books USA Inc.: From *Nature's Great Balancing Act in Our Own Backyard* by E. Jaediker Norsgaard, photographs by Campbell Norsgaard. Text copyright © 1990 by E. Jaediker Norsgaard; photographs copyright © 1990 by Campbell Norsgaard.

Fitzhenry & Whiteside, Limited, Markham, Ontario: *Wolf Island* by Celia Godkin. Copyright © 1989 by Celia Godkin.

Greenwillow Books, a division of William Morrow & Company, Inc.: Cover illustration by Jim Fowler from *Dolphin Adventure: A True Story* by Wayne Grover. Illustration copyright © 1990 by Jim Fowler. "I Am Flying" from *The New Kid on the Block* by Jack Prelutsky. Text copyright © 1984 by Jack Prelutsky.

Grosset & Dunlap, Inc., a division of The Putnam & Grosset Group: Cover illustration by Paige Billin-Frye from *What's Out There? A Book About Space* by Lynn Wilson. Illustration copyright © 1993 by Paige Billin-Frye.

Harcourt Brace & Company: Cover illustration by Greg Shed from *Dandelions* by Eve Bunting. Illustration copyright © 1995 by Greg Shed. *The Lotus Seed* by Sherry Garland, illustrated by Tatsuro Kiuchi. Text copyright © 1993 by Sherry Garland; illustrations copyright © 1993 by Tatsuro Kiuchi.

HarperCollins Publishers: *My Great-Aunt Arizona* by Gloria Houston, illustrated by Susan Condie Lamb. Text copyright © 1992 by Gloria Houston; illustrations copyright © 1992 by Susan Condie Lamb. "A Bug Sat in a Silver Flower" from *Dogs & Dragons, Trees & Dreams* by Karla Kuskin. Text copyright © 1975 by Karla Kuskin. Cover illustration by Kam Mak from *The Year of the Panda* by Miriam Schlein. Illustration copyright © 1990 by Kam Mak.

Holiday House, Inc.: *Wolves* by Gail Gibbons. Copyright © 1994 by Gail Gibbons.

Henry Holt and Company: Cover illustration by Cat Bowman Smith from *Max Malone Makes a Million* by Charlotte Herman. Illustration copyright © 1991 by Catherine Bowman Smith.

Houghton Mifflin Company: Cover illustration by Karen M. Dugan from *Halmoni and the Picnic* by Sook Nyul Choi. Illustration copyright © 1993 by Karen Milone Dugan. *When Jo Louis Won the Title* by Belinda Rochelle, illustrated by Larry Johnson. Text copyright © 1994 by Belinda Rochelle; illustrations copyright © 1994 by Larry Johnson. *Grandfather's Journey* by Allen Say. Copyright © 1993 by Allen Say.

Hyperion Books For Children: *All Eyes on the Pond* by Michael J. Rosen, illustrated by Tom Leonard. Text copyright © 1994 by Michael J. Rosen; illustrations © 1994 by Tom Leonard.

Alfred A. Knopf, Inc.: *Borreguita and the Coyote* by Verna Aardema, illustrated by Petra Mathers. Text copyright © 1991 by Verna Aardema; illustrations copyright © 1991 by Petra Mathers.

Larousse Kingfisher Chambers Inc., New York: From *Our Universe: A Guide To What's Out There* (Retitled: "Journey Through the Solar System") by Russell Stannard, illustrated by Michael Bennallack-Hart, Helen Floate, and Diana Mayo. Text copyright © 1995 by Russell Stannard; illustrations copyright © 1995 by Larousse plc.

Lee & Low Books, Inc.: Cover illustration by Cornelius Van Wright and Ying-Hwa Hu from *Sam and the Lucky Money* by Karen Chinn. Illustration copyright © 1995 by Cornelius Van Wright and Ying-Hwa Hu.

Lerner Publications Company, Minneapolis, MN: Cover photograph by Jake Rajs from *The Statue of Liberty: America's Proud Lady* by Jim Haskins. Copyright © 1986 by Jim Haskins.

Lothrop, Lee & Shepard Books, a division of William Morrow & Company, Inc.: *If You Made a Million* by David M. Schwartz, illustrated by Steven Kellogg. Text copyright © 1989 by David M. Schwartz; illustrations copyright © 1989 by Steven Kellogg; photographs of money copyright © 1989 by George Ancona.

Morrow Junior Books, a division of William Morrow & Company, Inc.: From *Ramona and Her Father* by Beverly Cleary. Text copyright © 1975, 1977 by Beverly Cleary. Cover illustration by Louis Darling from *Ellen Tebbits* by Beverly Cleary. Copyright 1951 by Beverly Cleary. Cover illustration by Alan Tiegreen from *Ramona the Brave* by Beverly Cleary. Copyright © 1975 by Beverly Cleary. Cover illustration by Louis Darling from *The Mouse and the Motorcycle* by Beverly Cleary. Copyright © 1965 by Beverly Cleary. Cover illustration by Beatrice Darwin from *Socks* by Beverly Cleary. Copyright © 1973 by Beverly Cleary. Cover illustration by Louis Darling from *Henry and the Clubhouse* by Beverly Cleary. Copyright © 1962 by Beverly Cleary. Cover illustration by Louis Darling from *Otis Spofford* by Beverly Cleary. Copyright © 1953 by Beverly Cleary. Cover illustration by Kay Life from *Muggie Maggie* by Beverly Cleary. Illustration copyright © 1990 by William Morrow and Company, Inc.

G. P. Putnam's Sons: From *Amber Brown Is Not a Crayon* by Paula Danziger, illustrated by Tony Ross. Text copyright © 1994 by Paula Danziger; illustrations copyright © 1994 by Tony Ross. Cover illustration by Tony Ross from *Amber Brown Goes Fourth* by Paula Danziger. Illustration copyright © 1995 by Tony Ross.

Random House, Inc.: Cover illustration by Dora Leder from *Julian's Glorious Summer* by Ann Cameron. Illustration copyright © 1987 by Dora Leder.

Marian Reiner, on behalf of Patricia Hubbell and Ju-Hong Chen: "The Inventor Thinks Up Helicopters" from *The Tigers Brought Pink Lemonade* by Patricia Hubbell, illustrated by Ju-Hong Chen. Text copyright © 1988 by Patricia Hubbell; illustration copyright © 1988 by Ju-Hong Chen.

Scholastic Inc.: Cover illustration from *All About Alligators* by Jim Arnosky. Copyright © 1994 by Jim Arnosky. From *My First Book of Biographies* (Retitled: "Creative Minds at Work") by Jean Marzollo. Text copyright © 1994 by Jean Marzollo.

Charles E. Tuttle Company, Inc.: "The King and the Poor Boy" from *Cambodian Folk Stories from the Gatiloke*, retold by Muriel Paskin Carrison, from a translation by The Venerable Kong Chhean. Text copyright © 1987 by Charles E. Tuttle Publishing Co., Inc.

Viking Penguin, a division of Penguin Books USA Inc.: Cover illustration by Susanna Natti from *Cam Jansen and the Mystery of the Television Dog* by David A. Adler. Illustration copyright © 1981 by Susanna Natti.

Dinh D. Vu: "Nothing that grows..."/ "Hoa Sen" from *The Lotus Seed* by Sherry Garland.

Walker Books Limited, London: Cover illustration from *When Hunger Calls* by Bert Kitchen. Copyright © 1994 by Bert Kitchen. Originally published in the United States by Candlewick Press, Cambridge, MA.

Photo Credits

Key: (t) top, (b) bottom, (c) center, (l) left, (r) right, (bg) background, (i) inset

John Lei/OPC, 18, 55, 199(bg), 200-201; Melody Norsgaard/Newcombe Productions, 64-65; Herb Segars/Animals Animals, 68; Stephen Dalton/Photo Researchers, 70; Art Wolfe/Tony Stone Images, 71; Dwight Kuhn/Bruce Coleman, Inc., 72; Laura Riley/Bruce Coleman, Inc. 73(t), 77(b); E. R. Degginger/Animals Animals, 73(b); W. Bayer/Bruce Coleman, Inc., 74-75; S. Nielsen/Bruce Coleman, Inc, 76; Joe McDonald/Animals Animals, 77(t); Phil Degginger/Bruce Coleman, Inc., 78; Keith Gunnar/Bruce Coleman, Inc, 78-79; Robert P. Carr/Bruce Coleman, Inc., 79; Sal DiMarco/Black Star/Harcourt Brace & Company, 104; Wes Bobbitt/Black Star/Harcourt Brace & Company, 127; Culver Pictures, 130-131(bg), 160-161(bg), 164-165(bg); Dale Higgins/Harcourt Brace & Company, 160; Bob Newey, 199; Dennis Brack/Black Star/Harcourt Brace & Company, 217(t); Rick Friedman/Black Star/Harcourt Brace & Company, 217(b) Richard B. Levine, 218(t), Debra P. Hershkowitz, 218(b); Jeff Greenberg/Photo Researchers, 219(t), 219(b); Superstock, 226-227, 229(i), 230, 236-237, 239(i), 246-247(b), 260(bg); Earl Young/FPG International, 228-229; Telegraph Colour Library/FPG International, 233, 234-235, 260(b); NASA, 235(i), 238-239, 243-245, 246, 247(b), 248-253, 261(t), 261(c). 261(b); David Hardy/Photo researchers, 254; the Bettmann Archive, 269, 271; Les Morsillo, 274-279

Illustration Credits

Gennady Spirin, Cover Art; Lori Lohstoeder, 6-7, 13-17, 108; Margaret Kasahara, 8-9, 109-110, 113, 220; Wayne Vincent, 10-11, 221-225, 332; Tyrone Geter, title page; Lehner & White, misc. icons; Petra Mathers, 18-37; Gail Gibbons, 38-51; Celia Godkin, 54-63; Tom Leonard, 64-69, 86-87, 92-93, 258-259; Kristin Goeters, 69; Daniel Moreton, 80-81; Tom Leonard, 84-107; Susan Condie Lamb, 114-129; Allen Say, 130-161, 164-165; Arvis Stewart, 161; Tatsuro Kiuchi, 166-187; Paula Danziger, 190-198, 200-201; Larry Johnson, 202-217; Tyrone Geter, 217; Tom Leonard, 256-257; Ju-Hong Chen, 258-295; Hugh Whyte, 268-271; Steven Kellogg, 278-313; R.J. Shay, 316-331